M c G R A W - H I L L
SCIENCE
M U S I C   C D
G R A D E S   K - 2

The Music CD contains songs in English and Spanish—over 40 songs in all. Use the songs to introduce science topics from the McGraw-Hill Science series of textbooks. The songs are referenced in the Teacher's Edition, and a complete correlation chart is found on pages 41 and 42 of this booklet.

Here is how to incorporate music into your science lessons:

- **PLAY** the song to your class.

- **SING** the song as a class. For children in Grades 1 and 2, you may wish to photocopy and distribute the song lyrics, which are found in this booklet. You may ask children to practice reading the song lyrics before singing them.

- **INTRODUCE** a science topic with a class activity or discussion, as presented in the Teaching Strategies section on pages 43–46.

CONTENTS

ENGLISH SONGS

SPANISH SONGS

Track and Title	Length	Page

My Oak Tree

I saw a little acorn,
Lying on the ground.
I put it in my pocket,
Told Daddy what I'd found.
He helped me plant it in the Earth,
Up came a little tree!
Just see what we have grown,
My Daddy and me!
An oak tree!

What Shall We Do On a Rainy Day?

What shall we do on a rainy day,
rainy day,
rainy day?
What shall we do on a rainy day,
When we can't go out to play?

The Arrival of Winter

Cold wind!
Hear how it blows!
Wind from north,
Cold winter's woes. (sss...)

Hail on the roof,
On the eaves,
On the trees.
Rat tat-a-tat
Hear the hail!
Watch it freeze.

Swirling and whirling,
It covers the ground.
Sifting and shifting
Snow falls without sound.

Sneaking, creeping,
Frost nips your nose!
Inch by inch
It nips at your toes.

Twinkle, Twinkle Little Star

Twinkle, twinkle little star,

How I wonder what you are!

Up above the world so high,

Like a diamond in the sky.

Twinkle, twinkle little star,

How I wonder what you are!

Jelly in the Bowl

Jelly in the bowl,

Jelly in the bowl,

Wiggle, waggle, wiggle, waggle,

Jelly in the bowl.

See-Saw

See-saw,

Up and down,

In the air,

And on the ground.

Johnny Works with One Hammer

Johnny works with one hammer,
One hammer, one hammer,
Johnny works with one hammer,
Then he works with two.

Johnny works with two hammers,
Two hammers, two hammers,
Johnny works with two hammers,
Then he works with three.

Johnny works with three hammers,
Three hammers, three hammers,
Johnny works with three hammers,
Then he works with four.

Johnny works with four hammers,
Four hammers, four hammers,
Johnny works with four hammers,
Then he works with five.

Johnny works with five hammers,
Five hammers, five hammers,
Johnny works with five hammers,
Then he works no more.

Mill Song

'Round and 'round,
The mill goes 'round.
As it does,
The corn is ground.

Engine, Engine, Number Nine

Engine, engine, number nine,
Going down the railroad line!
If the train goes off the track,
Will I get my money back?

Down at the Station

Down at the station,
Early in the morning,
See the little puffer billies all in a row.
See the engine driver pull the little handle.
Chug! Chug! Woo! Woo! Off we go.

I Have a Car

I have a car, it's made of tin.

Nobody knows what shape it's in.

It has four wheels and a rumble seat.

Hear us chugging down the street.

Honk honk rattle rattle rattle crash beep beep.

Honk honk rattle rattle rattle crash beep beep.

Honk honk rattle rattle rattle crash beep beep.

Honk honk.

Mr. Frog

On a log, Mister Frog
Sang a song the whole day long,
Glumph, Glumph, Glumph.

Shoo, Fly

Shoo, fly, don't bother me,
Shoo, fly, don't bother me,
Shoo, fly, don't bother me,
For I belong to somebody.

I feel, I feel, I feel,
I feel like a morning star,
I feel, I feel, I feel, I feel,
I feel like a morning star.

Oh, Shoo, fly, don't bother me,
Shoo, fly, don't bother me,
Shoo, fly, don't bother me,
For I belong to somebody.

Loose Tooth

I had a loose tooth, a
Wiggly, jiggly loose tooth,
I had a loose tooth,
Hanging by a thread.

So I pulled my loose tooth, this
Wiggly, jiggly loose tooth, and
Put it 'neath my pillow, and
Then I went to bed.

The fairies took my loose tooth, my
Wiggly, jiggly loose tooth, So
Now I have a quarter and a
Hole in my head.

Bluebells

Bluebells, cockle shells,
Eevy, ivy, overhead.
My mother said that I was born in
January, February, March, April,
May, June, July, August,
September, October, November, December.

Star Light, Star Bright

Star light, star bright,

First star I see tonight,

I wish I may,

I wish I might,

Have the wish I wish tonight.

Rain, Rain, Go Away

Rain, rain, go away.
Come again some other day.
Rain, rain, go away.
Little children want to play.

Bounce High, Bounce Low

Bounce high,
Bounce low,
Bounce the ball to Shiloh!

Is That the Sweet Sound?

Is that the sweet sound of music I hear?

Royal musicians passing so near?

Oh what can it be that I have heard?

Can it be? Can it be the sweet sound of a bird?

Yes, we can hear it so high and so clear.

Could it be that Spring is now here?

Yes, Spring has come to us once again.

And the coldness of Winter has come to an end.

The More We Get Together

The more we get together, together, together,
The more we get together, the happier we'll be!

For your friends are my friends,
And my friends are your friends,
The more we get together, the happier we'll be!

Mi hogar

Es mi casita querida, tan bonita como un Sol
es un hogar muy dichoso que me guarda con amor
allí están los que yo quiero, mi mamita y mi papá
mis hermanitos y abuelos. ¡Es mi hogar, un dulce hogar!

Los elefantes

Un elefante se balanceaba
sobre la tela de una araña,
y como ésta no se rompía,
fue a llamar a otro elefante.

Dos elefantes se balanceaban
sobre la tela de una araña,
y como ésta no se rompía,
fueron a llamar a otro elefante.

Tres elefantes…

Cuatro elefantes…

Cinco elefantes…

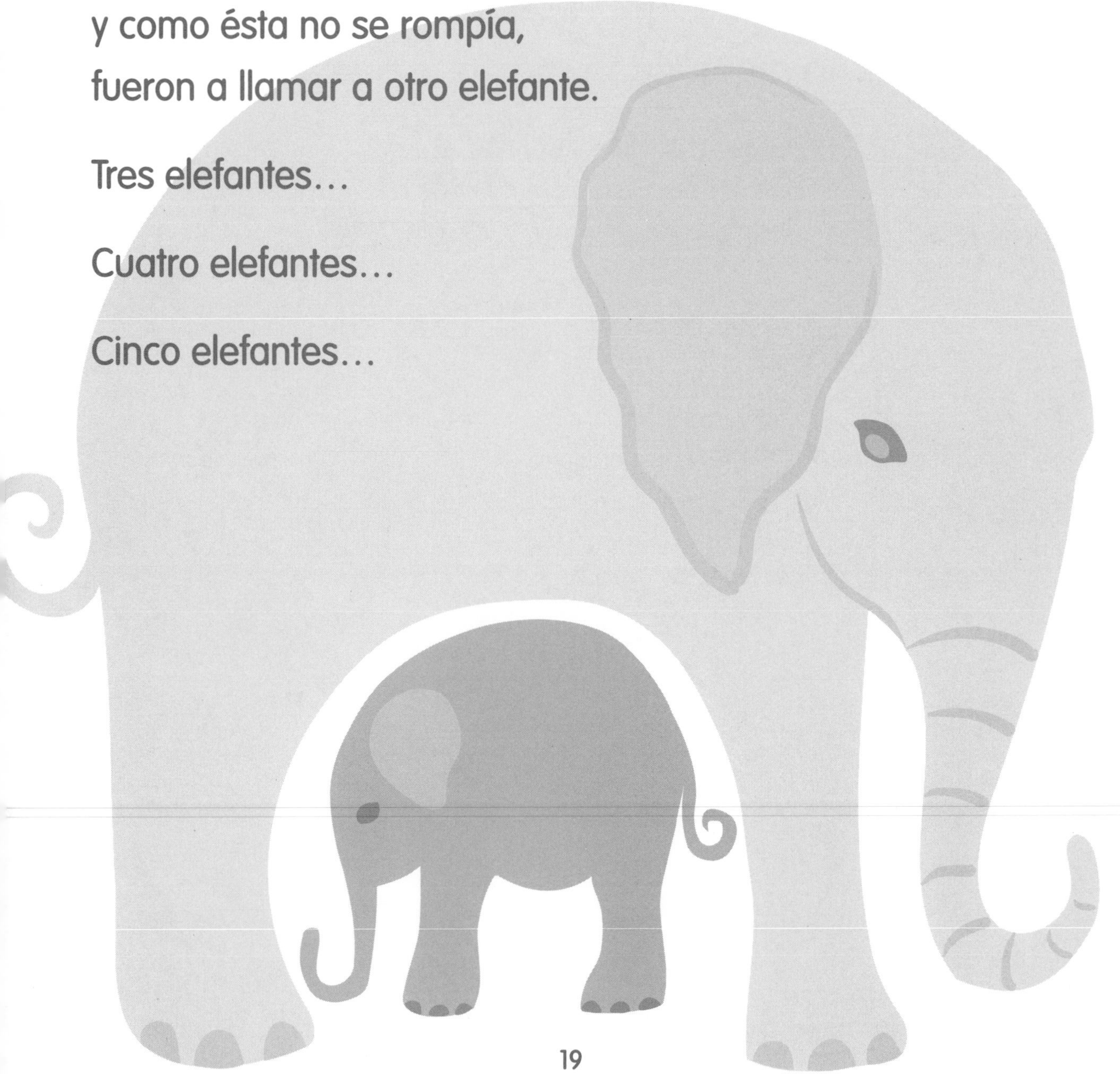

Yo tenía diez perritos

Yo tenía diez perritos,

yo tenía diez perritos,

uno no come ni bebe;

no me quedan más que nueve.

Los pollitos

Los pollitos dicen:
"Pío, pío, pío",
cuando tienen hambre,
cuando tienen frío.

La gallina busca
el maíz y el trigo,
les da la comida
y les preta abrigo.

Bajo sus dos alas,
acurrucaditos,
hasta el otro día
duermen los pollitos.

La canción del cucú

Llegó la primavera, el frío terminó.
Temprano esta mañana el cuclillo cantó.

¡Cucú! ¡Cucú!
¡Primavera llegó!
¡Cucú! Escucha y oirás la canción.

La nieve en la montaña, el sol la derritió.
Los pájaros regresan porque calienta el sol.

¡Cucú! ¡Cucú!
¡Primavera llegó!

Tengo una muñeca

Tengo una muñeca vestida de azul,

con su camisita y su canesú.

La saqué a paseo, se me resfrió.

La tengo en la cama con mucho dolor.

Dos y dos son cuatro, cuatro y dos son seis;

seis y dos son ocho y ocho dieciséis;

y ocho, veinticuatro y ocho, treinta y dos.

Ánimas benditas me arrodillo yo.

Riqui ran

Aserrín, aserrán,

los maderos de San Juan,

comen queso, comen pan.

Los de Rique alfeñique;

los de Roque alfandoque.

Riqui, rique, riqui, ran.

La bella hortelana

Cuando siembra la bella hortelana;
cuando siembra, siembra así.
Si siembra poco a poco,
luego pone las manos así.
Riega así, corta así.

Cuando riega la bella hortelana,
cuando riega, riega así.
Si riega poco a poco,
luego pone las manos así,
riega así, siembra así.
Luego pone las manos así.

Cuando corte la bella hortelana,
cuando corta, corta así.
Si corta poco a poco,
luego pone las manos así,
corta así, riega así, siembra así.
Luego pone las manos así.

Las mañanitas

Éstas son las mañanitas que cantaba el Rey David,
pero no eran tan bonitas como las cantan aquí.

Despierta, mi bien, despierta, mira que ya amaneció,
ya los pajarillos cantan, la luna ya se metió.

El zapatero

Yo le dije al zapatero
que me hiciera unos zapatos
con el pico redondito
como los que usan los patos.

¡Malhaya el zapatero!
Cómo me engañó;
me hizo los zapatos,
pero el piquito, ¡no!

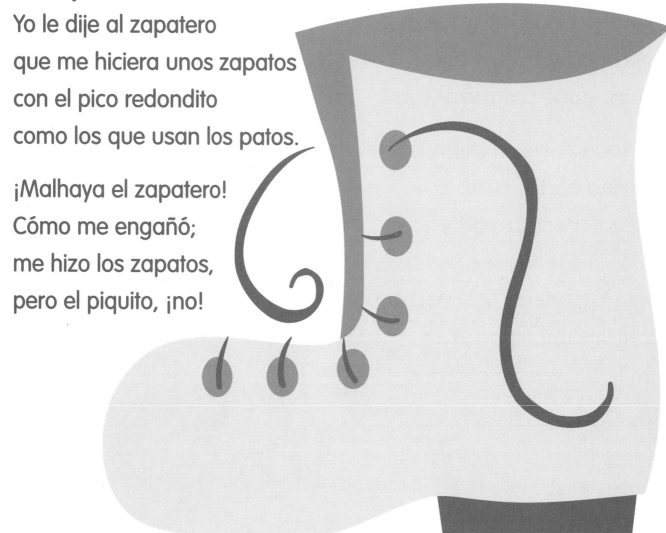

La gente de tu vecindario

¡Oh! Cuánta gente hay en tu vecindario,
(en tu) vecindario, (en tu) vecindario.
Cuánta gente hay en tu vecindario.
¡Oh! Cuánta gente puedes ver.

El cartero siempre muy contento
con lluvia, con sol o con viento.
Él lleva de aquí para allá
las cartas que él reparti…

El cartero en tu vecindario,
(en tu) vecindario, (en tu) vecindario.
El cartero en tu vecindario
es alguien a quien puedes ver.

El bombero cumple su misión
montado en rojo camión
donde haya un incendio irá
y seguro que lo apagará.

El bombero en tu vecindario,
(en tu) vecindario, (en tu) vecindario.
El bombero en tu vecindario
es alguien a quien puedes ver.
Cuando salgas a pasear,
en tu vecindario ves pasar.

La mar estaba serena

La mar estaba serena,
serena estaba la mar;
la mar estaba serena,
serena estaba la mar.

Li mir istibi sirini,
sirini istibi li mir;
li mir istibi sirini,
sirini istibi li mir.

La mar astaba sarana,
sarana astaba la mar;
la mar astaba sarana,
sarana astaba la mar.

Lo mor ostobo sorono,
sorono ostobo lo mor;
lo mor ostobo sorono,
sorono ostobo lo mor.

Le mer estebe serene,
serene estebe le mer;
le mer estebe serene,
serene estebe le mer.

Lu mur ustubu surunu,
surunu ustubu lu mur;
lu mur ustubu surunu,
surunu ustubu lu mur.

Hombros y cabeza

Hombros y cabeza, uno, dos, tres.

Hombros y cabeza, uno, dos, tres.

Hombros y cabeza y hombros y cabeza, baby,

uno, dos, tres.

Rodilla y tobillo, uno, dos, tres.

Rodilla y tobillo, uno, dos, tres.

Rodilla y tobillo y rodilla y tobillo, baby,

uno, dos, tres.

Ordeña la vaca ....

Tira la pelota ....

El Florón

El florón está en las manos,
y en las manos está el florón.
Adivinen quién lo tiene,
o se queda da plantón.

In my hand is a lovely flower,
Pretty flower I hold in my hand.
Now, I wonder who will have it,
Or will it stay in my hand?

El gran Washington

A Washington el grande, tú lo debes conocer.
A los indios y franceses en los lagos combatió.

Cuando Jorge de Inglaterra impuso la opresión,
Washington el grande luchó por la libertad.

Llegó a ser el primer gran presidente del país
y por todos respetado con honor y admiración.

Cantemos todos juntos, hoy gritemos su lección
de amar a nuestra patria y de respetar el bien.

También amó a los niños, hasta los llevó a pasear
y tiró un dólar de plata en el ancho Rappahannock.

Al morir lo enterraron junto al río Potomac
y un mármol en su tumba honra al héroe nacional.

A Washington el grande, hoy debemos emular
y mañana cuando grandes, ser tan grandes como él.

El barco chiquitito

Había una vez un barco chiquitito,
había una vez un barco chiquitito,
había una vez un barco chiquitito,
que no podía, que no podía,
que no podía navegar.

Pasaron una, dos, tres, cuatro, cinco,
seis, siete semanas.
Pasaron una, dos, tres, cuatro, cinco,
seis, siete semanas.
Pasaron una, dos, tres, cuatro, cinco,
seis, siete semanas, y los víveres, y los víveres,
empezaron a escasear.

Cada vez que nos juntamos

Cada vez que nos juntamos, juntamos, juntamos,
cada vez que nos juntamos, alegres nos ven.
Tu amigo es mi amigo y mi amigo es tu amigo,
cada vez que nos juntamos, alegres nos ven.

Corre trenecito corre

Chuchu chucu chucu.
Chuchu chucu chucu.

Corre trenecito, corre ya quiero empezar a contemplar,
corre trenecito corre ya quiero escuchar tu chucu chu.

Quiero recorrer los montes y al viento acariciar,
quiero contemplar los valles y el lago de cristal,
quierro ver passar las vacas con cencerro sin cencerro
que me gustan tanto a mí.

Pienso que tu vas comiendo a pesar de ir
corriendo y lo llevas todo en ti.

Corre trenecito, corre ya quiero llegar a mi ciudad,
corre trenecito corre pues quiero a mis amigos platicar.

Como devoras distancias con ritmo musical.
Como saludas los campos con tu canto chucu chu,
y en alegre recorrido voy cantando voy
contigo pues me siento muy feliz
de que seas mi buen amigo trenecito
que contento vas a gran velocidad.

Todos los nacidos en enero

Todos los de enero tienen que saltar
con un pie primero y el otro después.
Tra la la la la la, tra la la la la la la.
Todos los de enero tienen que saltar.

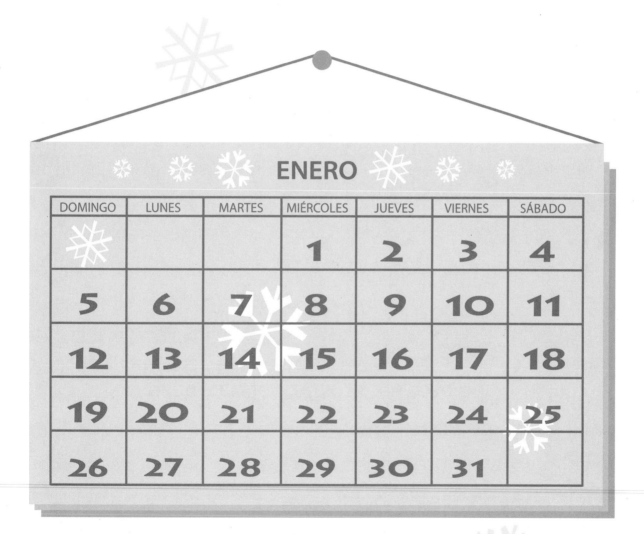

DOMINGO	LUNES	MARTES	MIÉRCOLES	JUEVES	VIERNES	SÁBADO
			1	2	3	4
5	6	7	8	9	10	11
12	13	14	15	16	17	18
19	20	21	22	23	24	25
26	27	28	29	30	31	

ENERO

La bamba

Para bailar la bamba,
para bailar la bamba se necesita
una poca de gracia,
una poca de gracia y otra cosita
y arriba y arriba,
y arriba y arriba y arriba iré,
por ti seré, por ti seré.

Bamba, bamba.
Bamba, bamba.
Bamba, bamba.

Bamba, cielo,
para subir al cielo se necesita
una escalera grande,
una escalera grande y otra chiquita
y arriba y arriba,
y arriba y arriba y arriba iré,
por ti seré, por ti seré.

La montaña

Cuando estés en la montaña, cuando estés allá,
cuando estés en la montaña, síentate a llorar.

Sí, sí, sí, acuérdate de mí.
Sí, sí, sí, acuérdate de mí.

Valle lindo, valle lindo, valle lindo allá,
canta suave y muy lento, canta con amor.

Tempestuoso grande y ancho, tempestuoso mar,
no te puedes esconder en ese mar azul.

Vamos a la mar

Vamos a la mar, tum tum,
a comer pescado, tum tum;
boca colorada, tum tum,
fritito y asado, tum tum.

Let's go to the sea, tum tum,
We will eat some fishes, tum tum;
Boca colorada, tum tum,
Fried and hot and spicy, tum tum.

Mi Cuerpo

Mi cuerpo, mi cuerpo hace música,
Mi cuerpo, mi cuerpo hace música.

Mis manos hacen (clap clap clap),
mis pies hacen (stamp stamp stamp),
mi boca hace "La, la, la,"
mi cuerpo hace "Cha cha cha."

ENGLISH SONGS

KINDERGARTEN

Learn About Your World
19. Is That the Sweet Sound? **TOPIC 2**
5. Jelly in the Bowl **TOPIC 3**

Learn About Plants
1. My Oak Tree **TOPIC 4**

Learn About Animals
12. Mr. Frog **TOPIC 3**

A Home Called Earth
8. Mill Song **TOPIC 5**

Weather and Seasons
2. What Shall We Do on a Rainy Day? **TOPIC 1**
17. Rain, Rain, Go Away **TOPIC 1**
3. The Arrival of Winter **TOPIC 6**
15. Bluebells **TOPIC 6**

Make Things Move
6. See-Saw **TOPIC 2**
7. Johnny Works With One Hammer **TOPIC 2**
8. Mill Song **TOPIC 4**
9. Engine, Engine, Number Nine **TOPIC 4**

GRADE 1

A Tree
1. My Oak Tree **TOPIC 6**

The Sky
2. What Shall We Do On a Rainy Day? **TOPIC 3**
3. The Arrival of Winter **TOPIC 4**
4. Twinkle, Twinkle, Little Star **TOPIC 6**

Matter, Matter Everywhere
5. Jelly in the Bowl **TOPIC 1**

On the Move
6. See-Saw **TOPIC 1**
7. Johnny Works With One Hammer **TOPIC 1**
8. Mill Song **TOPIC 2**
9. Engine, Engine, Number Nine **TOPIC 2**
10. Down At the Station **TOPIC 3**
11. I Have a Car **TOPIC 3**

A Pond
12. Mr Frog **TOPIC 4**
13. Shoo, Fly **TOPIC 5**

Human Body: Being You
14. Loose Tooth **TOPIC 1**

GRADE 2

Watering Earth's Plants
15. Bluebells **TOPIC 1**
17. Rain, Rain Go Away **TOPIC 5**

Changes All Around
16. Star Light, Star Bright **TOPIC 4**
19. Is That the Sweet Sound? **TOPIC 5**

Watch It Move
18. Bounce High, Bounce Low **TOPIC 2**

Human Body: Heart and Lungs
20. The More We Get Together **TOPIC 3**

SPANISH SONGS

KINDERGARTEN

Conoce tu mundo
21. Mi hogar TEMA 1
26. Tengo una muñeca TEMA 1

Aprende sobre las plantas
34. El florón TEMA 3
28. La bella hortelana TEMA 4

Aprende sobre los animales
22. Los elefantes TEMA 4
23. Yo tenía diez perritos TEMA 5
24. Los pollitos TEMA 5

Mi hogar: la Tierra
41. La montaña TEMA 1

El tiempo y las estaciones
25. La canción del cucú TEMA 5

Haz que se mueva
36. El barco chiquitito TEMA 6

GRADO 1

El árbol
28. La bella hortelana TEMA 2

Materia y más materia
30. El zapatero TEMA 1

En movimiento
31. La gente de tu vecindario TEMA 4
33. Hombros y cabeza TEMA 5

El estanque
32. La mar estaba serena TEMA 6

El cuerpo humano: cómo eres
26. Tengo una muñeca TEMA 1
33. Hombros y cabeza TEMA 1
39. Todos los nacidos en Enero TEMA 1

GRADO 2

Las plantas y el agua
34. El florón TEMA 1

Todo cambia
36. El barco chiquitito TEMA 6

¿Cómo se mueve?
38. Corre trenecito corre TEMA 1

La vida en las rocas
41. La montaña TEMA 2

El cuerpo humano: corazón y pulmones
37. Cada vez que nos juntamos TEMA 3
43. Mi cuerpo TEMA 3

Acknowledgments

Mi hogar
Isis Pérez de Méndes-Peñate; María Luisa Muñoz

La gente de tu vecindario
Letra y música de JEFFREY MOSS. LA GENTE DE TU VECINDARIO, traducción de THE PEOPLE IN YOUR NEIGHBORHOOD. Copyright 1969 de Festival Attractions. Reservados todos los derechos, includios los internacionales.

Corre trenecito corre
Letra y música de Elba Rodríguez

Todos los nacidos en enero
Publicada en MUSIC AND YOU, Book 3, Barbara Stanton y Merrill Stanton, Senior Authors. Copyright © 1988 de Macmillan Publishing Company, una división de Macmillan, Inc.

La bamba
Publicada en CANTEMOS EN ESPAÑOL, Libro II (K1 12). © Copyright 194, renovado en 1975, Max y Beatrice Krone. Distribuido por Neil A. Kjos Music Company, San Diego, California. Impresión autorizada 1988.

ENGLISH SONGS

MY OAK TREE
Learning Through Movement

children develop movements on the theme of growth by hav-
them imagine what it would be like to be an acorn growing into
ighty oak tree. As they listen to the song, encourage children to
ut the motions of seeing an acorn, putting it in their pocket,
planting the acorn, as well as the acorn growing into a tree.

CUSSION

hat is an acorn? (An acorn is a seed that might grow into an
k tree.)

hat does an acorn need to grow into an oak tree? (An acorn
eds to be planted in the ground, as well as water and sunlight.)

WHAT SHALL WE DO ON A RAINY DAY?
Art Connection

children work in groups to make pictures that illustrate rain,
as:

rain in the city,
rain on a farm,
rain at the beach,
umbrellas,
rain clothes,
staying indoors on a rainy day.

may choose to have children create collages, using construction
er, glue, and bits of torn paper. Or, cut out large raindrop
es from heavy construction paper, and have children draw their
res on these shapes.

CUSSION

o you enjoy rainy days? (accept all answers.)

hy is rain important? (Rain waters plants, washes away dirt,
d collects in ponds, lakes, and rivers. Earth would dry up with-
t rain.)

THE ARRIVAL OF WINTER
Theatrical Reading

de the class into four groups, one for each section of "The
val of Winter". In each group, have one child speak the words,
e the others mime the weather being described. Give children
e to rehearse. Then, stage "The Arrival of Winter" as a theatrical
ling.

CUSSION

o you like winter? Why? (Accept all answers.)

hat happens in winter? (In many places, the temperature
comes very cold, frost forms, and snow falls.)

TWINKLE, TWINKLE, LITTLE STAR
Visual Learning

n the shades or blinds, and turn on all of the lights in the class-
m. Ask a volunteer to aim a flashlight at the chalkboard. Ask
dren what they see there. Then, turn off the lights one at a time,
gradually close the shades or blinds. Have children describe
the light from the flashlight changes.

CUSSION

hen could you best see the light from the flashlight? (The

light was easiest to see when there was no other lights in the
room.)

- When can you see stars? (Only at night.)
- Why can you see stars only at night? (During the day, the light
  from the sun is so bright it hides the light from stars.)

5. **JELLY IN THE BOWL**
   ### Language Arts Connection

Have students think of other things that might be in a bowl. Then,
make up rhymes like "Jelly in the Bowl" that fit these things. A
rhyme for water, for example, could be:

Water in the bowl
Water in the bowl
Splish, splash, splish, splash,
Water in the bowl.

DISCUSSION

- What is jelly like? (Jelly is soft, squishy, sticky, and tastes sweet.)
- Name something that is soft and squishy, but doesn't taste
  sweet. (Possible answers are glue, a sponge, and cotton.)

6. **SEE-SAW**
   ### Learning through Movement

Divide the class into pairs. Have each pair explore ways to move
their bodies like a see-saw. For example, two children might join
hands, rock back and forth, and try to counterbalance each other
without tipping over.

DISCUSSION

- How did you pretend to be a see-saw? (Accept all answers.)
- How do see-saws work? (A child at one end of the see-saw pushes
  down on the ground, lifting himself up as the other child falls.)
- In science, what is the name for a push or a pull? (A push or
  pull is called a force.)

7. **JOHNNY WORKS WITH ONE HAMMER**
   ### Learning through Movement

Have children move their body parts in time to the music. For the
words "one hammer," have them pound one fist as if it were a hammer. For "two hammers," have them pound two fists. Then add one
foot, then two feet, and then the head.

DISCUSSION

- Does a hammer move on its own? (No, someone must move the
  hammer.)
- How does a hammer work? (A person moves the hammer so it
  strikes a nail, which pounds the nail into something.)
- Why might a hammer be dangerous? (If the hammer misses the
  nail, it could strike someone's thumb.)

8. **THE MILL SONG**
   ### Art Connection

Explain that mills are used to grind grains, such as corn, wheat,
oats, and rice. Today, grain is ground in factories, where machines
produce huge amounts of flour. But in some cultures, people still
grind grain by hand for their daily meals. Encourage children to
look up pictures of mills in an encyclopedia or other reference
source.

Have children draw pictures of their favorite foods that contain
grains. These foods might include corn-on-the-cob, tacos, sandwich-
es, oatmeal, or rice pudding.

9. ENGINE, ENGINE, NUMBER NINE
Language Arts Connection

Have children list other machines that take you from one place to another. The list might include cars, buses, boats, and airplanes. As a class, make up rhymes in the style of "Engine, Engine, Number Nine" for each of these machines. For an airplane, for example, a rhyme could be as follows:

> Airplane, airplane, number eight,
> We think you are really great.
> If the plane flies very low,
> We might see a buffalo!

DISCUSSION
- **What do cars, buses, trains, and planes have in common?** (All move quickly from place to place, much faster than people could move by themselves.)
- **When would you take a trip in a car? A bus? A train? An airplane?** (People use cars to go around town or on long trips. Buses and trains help move lots of people, which is important in big cities. Airplanes move very fast, and are quick ways of traveling long distances.)

10. DOWN AT THE STATION
(also **38. Corre trenecito corre**)
Art Connection

Discuss with the class the different kinds of cars that could make up a train, such as passenger cars, box cars, flat cars, tank cars, and livestock cars, as well as the locomotive and caboose. Next, have each child draw a railroad car. Or, teams of children could work together to create a model railroad car, perhaps using cardboard boxes, heavy construction paper, and rods or pencils for the axles of the wheels. When the children are finished, hook the cars together with yarn and masking tape to create a model train.

DISCUSSION
- **¿Han viajado alguna vez por tren? ¿Les gustó?** (Acepte todas las respuestas).
- **¿Cuáles son las partes de un tren?** (Un tren tiene una locomotora al frente, seguida de muchos coches. El último podría ser el vagón de cola).
- **¿En qué se diferencia un automóvil de un tren?** (Un automóvil es un coche cuyo conductor puede dirigirlo en cualquier dirección. Un tren tiene muchos coches y debe permanecer en los rieles).
- *Have you ever ridden on a train? What was it like? (Accept all answers.)*
- *What are the parts of a train? (A train has a locomotive in front, followed by many cars. The last car could be a caboose.)*
- *How is an automobile different from a train? (An automobile is a car that its driver can steer in any direction. A train has many cars, and must stay on the rails.)*

11. I HAVE A CAR
History Connection

Explain that cars do not have rumble seats today, but rumble seats were popular in cars in the late 1920s and early 1930s. These cars had no back seat; however, the trunk folded out to make a seat for two. Passengers had to climb onto the bumper and over the fender to get in place for a ride.

Have children look through old magazines, picture books, or other reference sources for pictures of different types of cars. If possible, have them cut out the pictures and glue them onto poster board to make a car display. Encourage them to look for old models, as well as newer ones.

DISCUSSION
- **What do all cars have in common?** (Cars are machines that move from place to place. They have wheels, an engine, and room for passengers and cargo. Most cars are made of steel.)
- **How can cars be different from one another?** (Cars have been built in different shapes, sizes, and colors. They can have different numbers of doors, windows, seats, and other parts.)

12. MR. FROG
Language Arts Connection

Work with the class to create rhymes for other animals in the style of "Mr. Frog". For example, here is a rhyme for a bear:

> Look who's there,
> Mister bear.
> He eats his fish
> And has thick hair.
> Growl, growl, growl.

DISCUSSION
- **What different noises do animals make?** (Accept all reasonable answers.)
- **Why do you think animals make noise?** (In many cases, animals make noises to communicate--the same reason that people make noises.)

13. SHOO, FLY
Kinesthetic Learning

Have children listen to the song, then sing it with the CD. Then, introduce movements to accompany specific song lyrics. Have children stand up. For the word "fly", have them flap their hands, keeping elbows at the side. For "belong to somebody", have them cross their arms and sway back and forth. For "morning star", have them spread their arms and legs apart, forming the points of a star.

DISCUSSION
- **What kind of animal is a fly?** A fly is a small, flying insect. Flies can be annoying, but usually they do not harm us.
- **What other animals fly?** Many birds and insects fly. So do bats.
- **Why are these animals able to fly?** They have wings that they can move very fast. Also, their bodies are shaped for flight, and they are lightweight.

14. LOOSE TOOTH
Art Connection

Have children draw pictures to illustrate a scene from the speech piece. You may choose to make and distribute templates in the shape of a tooth.

DISCUSSION
- **Who has had a loose tooth? What was it like? Did it come out?** (Accept all answers)
- **Why do children's teeth fall out?** Children's teeth fall out to make way for adult teeth, which are permanent.
- **Does the tooth fairy really exist?** No. Maybe a parent or guardian pretends to be the tooth fairy.
- **How can you take care of your teeth?** Brush your teeth regularly, floss after meals, and see your dentist.

15. BLUEBELLS
Art Connection

Have children choose their favorite months, or assign one month each child. Then, ask children to draw a picture that illustrates the month. Alternatively, children may create posters, collages, or dioramas.

ange the finished art on the walls or around the classroom to
w the cycle of seasons. As a class, review the art and discuss how
changes from month to month.

CUSSION
- hat's the weather like in January and February? (The weather
  cold. It is snowy in the north and on mountains.)
- hat's the weather like in July and August? (The weather is
  ot. In some places it is rainy. In other places it is very dry.)

STAR LIGHT, STAR BRIGHT
Art Connection
e children draw pictures of stars in the night sky. Alternatively,
may create posters, collages, or dioramas.

CUSSION
- hat do stars look like at night? (In the night sky, they look like
  ny, dim points of light.)
- hy can't you see stars during the day? (The Sun is so bright, it
  vers up the light of the stars. In fact, the Sun is a star. If we
  uld get closer to other stars, most would look more like the Sun.)
- ave you ever made a wish on a star? Did the wish come true?
  ccept all answers.)

RAIN, RAIN, GO AWAY
Art Connection
e children work in groups to make pictures that illustrate rain,
as:

rain in the city,
rain on a farm,
rain at the beach,
umbrellas,
rain clothes,
staying indoors on a rainy day.

may choose to have children create collages, using construction
er, glue, and bits of torn paper. Or, cut out large raindrop
pes from heavy construction paper, and have children draw their
ures on these shapes.

CUSSION
- o you enjoy rainy days? (accept all answers.)
- hy is rain important? (Rain waters plants, washes away dirt,
  nd collects in ponds, lakes, and rivers. Earth would dry up with-
  t rain.)

BOUNCE HIGH, BOUNCE LOW
Kinesthetic Learning: Ball Call
e children stand in a circle, with one child in the middle holding
astic ball. The child in the middle calls the name of another
d, throws the ball straight up, then moves out of the way. The
d who was called tries to catch the ball before it reaches the
nd or floor. If the child is successful, he or she replaces the
wer. If not, the thrower gets another turn.

teacher may need to designate limits for what constitutes a fair
. The teacher should select children to be called or to be the
wer so that all children have a turn in the game.

CUSSION
- hen you throw a ball into the air, why does it come down?
  he ball comes back to the ground by the force of gravity.)
- ow fast is the ball moving when it's highest? (If the ball was
  rown straight up, and if it doesn't hit the ceiling or another
  oject, then it won't be moving at all for a brief instant at the very
  p of the throw. Look carefully at a thrown ball to try to see this.)

19. IS THAT THE SWEET SOUND?
DISCUSSION
- **What is making the "sweet sound" in the song?** (A bird is making the sound.)
- **Why do bird songs mean that winter is over and spring has
  begun?** (In places where the winter is cold, most birds fly to
  warmer places for the winter. When spring comes, the weather
  becomes warmer and the birds return.)
- **Why do you think birds sing?** (Singing is how birds talk to one
  another.)

20. THE MORE WE GET TOGETHER
(also **37. Cada vez que nos juntamos**)
Group Learning

Have children sit in a circle and play the song to the class. Then,
have the class sing the song one word at a time. (ie, go around the
circle and have each child sing only one word.) Next, have pairs of
children sing two words together, then have groups of four children
sing four words, then groups of eight children sing eight words, and
so on until you are ready for the entire class to sing the whole song
together.

DISCUSSION
- **De todas las maneras de cantar la canción, ¿cuál les gustó
  más?** (Acepte todas las respuestas).
- **¿Cómo se sienten más contentos: en grupos grandes, en grupos
  pequeños o solos?** (Estimule a los niños a entender que hay
  muchas respuestas a esta pregunta. En ocasiones tal vez quieran
  estar en grupos y en otros momentos quizás sientan la necesidad
  de estar solos).
- *Which way of singing the song did you like best? (Accept all
  answers.)*
- *Are you happier in big groups, in small groups, or by yourself?
  (Encourage children to see that there are many answers to this question.
  Sometimes they may want to be in groups, and sometimes they may
  want to be alone.)*

SPANISH SONGS

21. MI HOGAR (MY HOUSE)
Art Connection
Have children draw a house that has several different rooms.
Children may choose to draw their own house, the house of a friend
or relative, or a house of their imagination. Have children label the
different rooms of the house.

DISCUSSION
- **Nombren algunos de los diferentes tipos de habitaciones
  en una casa.** (Las respuestas incluyen la cocina, la sala y el
  dormitorio).
- **Si pudieran construir su casa propia, ¿qué clase de habitaciones elegirían?** (Acepte todas las respuestas).
- *Name some of the different kinds of rooms in a house. (Answers
  include kitchen, living room, dining room, and bedroom.)*
- *If you could build your own house, what kind of rooms would you
  choose? (Accept all answers)*

22. LOS ELEFANTES (THE ELEPHANTS)
Science Background

Elephants are the largest, heaviest animals that live on land. (Some
whales, which live in the oceans, are larger.) Although elephants

are common in zoos and circuses, elephants in the wild are endangered. This means their numbers are so low that they might not survive. One reason for their low numbers is that they are hunted for their tusks, which are made of a valuable substance called ivory.

Have children learn more about elephants from books, encyclopedias, or the Internet. Ask children to share what they learn with the class.

23. YO TENÍA DIEZ PERRITOS (I HAD TEN PUPPIES)
Art Connection

Have children draw pictures to illustrate ten puppies. You may choose to have each child draw only one puppy, then combine the drawings for a class set.

24. LOS POLLITOS (THE CHICKS)
Art Connection

Have children make puppets of chicks to accompany the singing of this song. One simple way to make a chick puppet is to draw a chick head and body on a paper plate. Then, use a children's safety scissors (round-tipped cutting blades) to cut a slit where the beak would be. Insert the scissors' blades through the slit to model the beak.

DISCUSSION
- ¿Qué es un pollito o polluelo? (Un pollito o un polluelo es un bebé de gallina. Irá creciendo hasta convertirse en una gallina).
- *What is a chick? (A chick is a baby chicken. It will grow into a chicken as it gets older.)*

25. LA CANCIÓN DEL CUCÚ (THE SONG OF THE CUCU CLOCK)
Background Information

People have always been interested in measuring time. In many ancient cultures, people built sundials to tell the time during the day. Sundials work because the sun casts shadows in different directions as it moves across the sky.

The length of a day comes from nature: It is the time from sunrise to sunrise. But the division of a day into hours, minutes, and seconds is a human idea. Today, most people on Earth divide a day into 24 hours, an hour into 60 minutes, and a minute into 60 seconds.

Cucu clocks are a fun way to measure time. Have children imagine their own humorous or unusual kind of clock. Possible ideas are a clock that makes different sounds on the hour or half-hour, displays the time in an interesting way, or tells more than just the time. Have children draw a picture of their idea for a clock.

26. TENGO UNA MUÑECA (I HAVE A DOLL)
Art Connection

Have children design and create a doll of their own. Tell the children that their dolls should have eyes, ears, a mouth, a nose, two arms, and two legs. Children may make their dolls from construction paper and crayons, or for more elaborate dolls, felt pieces or remnants of old clothes. Arranged the finished dolls around the classroom walls.

28. LA BELLA HORTELANA (THE PRETTY GARDENER)

DISCUSSION
- ¿Tienen jardín dónde viven? (Acepte todas las respuestas).
- ¿Qué es lo que pueden cultivar en un jardín? (Las plantas crecen en jardines. La mayoría de los jardineros eligen plantas que tienen flores hermosas, o que producen verduras o frutas que podemos comer).

- ¿Qué deben hacer para que las plantas sigan creciendo? (La plantas necesitan ser regadas y que se les mantenga sin malas hierbas o maleza. Las sustancias químicas especiales llamadas tilizantes que se les agrega, ayudan a las plantas a crecer. El añadirles otro tipo de sustancias químicas aleja a los insectos dañinos y otras pestes).
- *Do you have a garden where you live? (Accept all answers)*
- *What sort of things can you grow in a garden? (Plants grow in gardens. Most gardeners choose plants that have pretty flowers, or make vegetables or fruits that we can eat.)*
- *What work must you do to keep plants growing? (Plants need t watered and kept free of weeds. Adding special chemicals called fert ers help plants grow. Adding other chemicals keeps away harmful insects and other pests.)*

30. EL ZAPATERO (THE SHOEMAKER)
Art Connection

Have each child draw a picture of a shoe. Encourage children to their imaginations and be unique. The goal for the class is to dr as many different shoes as possible.

When the children are finished, show each picture to the class. A class, decide upon a word that applies to each shoe. The word co apply to the shoe's color (brown, red, white), size (big, small, tall short), feel (hard, soft, fuzzy), or other attribute. Write the word o the picture, and tape the pictures on the classroom wall.

DISCUSSION
- ¿Qué tienen en común todos los zapatos? (Todos calzan bien, deberían calzar bien en los pies de las personas).
- ¿En qué se diferencian los zapatos entre sí? (Los zapatos vien en tamaños, formas y colores diferentes, y pueden estar hechos distintos materiales. Algunos tienen hebillas y otros traen lacit
- *What do all shoes have in common? (They all fit, or should fit, o people's feet.)*
- *How are shoes different from one another? (Shoes can come in d ferent sizes, shapes, and colors, and can be made of different mater Some have buckles, others have laces.)*

31. LA GENTE DE TU VECINDARIO
(THE PEOPLE IN YOUR NEIGHBORHOOD)

DISCUSSION
- ¿Qué clases de trabajos realizan las personas en sus vecinda ios? (Acepte todas las respuestas).
- ¿Y los otros seres vivos, además de las personas? ¿Qué hacen en sus vecindarios? (Guíe a los niños a entender de que todos seres vivos juegan un papel en sus vecindarios. Los árboles proporcionan refugio y a veces frutos. Las abejas esparcen el polen flor en flor. Muchos pájaros comen insectos, reduciendo el núm de éstos. Los gusanos y las bacterias viven en la tierra, y mantienen la tierra saludable para las plantas).
- *What jobs do people have in your neighborhood? (Accept all answers.)*
- *How about other living things, besides people? What do they d in your neighborhood? (Lead students to see that all living things play a role in their neighborhood. Trees provide shelter, and sometim fruit. Bees spread pollen from flower to flower. Many birds eat insec which keep the insects' numbers low. Worms and bugs live in the so and keep the soil healthy for plants.)*

32. LA MAR ESTABA SERENA (THE SEA IS SERENE) and
42. VAMOS A LA MAR (LET'S GO TO THE SEA)
Kinesthetic Learning

ve children create movements of things they would do at the
ch or on a boat, and then do these movements to the steady beat
hey sing the song. Or, they could create movements to show
an waves, or fishes.

CUSSION

Han visto un océano? ¿Cómo era? (Acepte todas las respuestas).
Qué cosas viven en el océano? (Los océanos son los hogares de
uchos animales, entre los que se incluyen almejas, calamares,
eces, delfines y ballenas. También es el hogar de las algas mari-
as).
ave you seen an ocean? What was it like? (Accept all answers.)
*What things live in the ocean? (Oceans are home to many animals,
cluding clams, squids, fishes, dolphins, and whales. It is also home to
lgae and seaweed.)*

HOMBROS Y CABEZA (HEAD AND SHOULDERS) and
MI CUERPO (MY BODY)
Language Arts Connection

these songs to teach the Spanish words for body parts:

Body is cuerpo (kwer-po).
Hands are manos (ma-nos).
Feet are pies (py-es).
Mouth is boca (bo-ka).
Head is hombros (ohm-bros)
Shoulder is cabeza (ka-bay-za)

CUSSION

Les gusta hacer música? ¿Por qué? (Acepte todas las respuestas)
De qué otras maneras la gente hace música? (Las personas a
enudo usan instrumentos musicales tales como pianos, tam-
ores, trompetas, clarinetes y muchos más. La gente puede hacer
do tipo de sonidos con un instrumento musical, con sólo soplar
mover sus manos).
Do you like making music? Why? (Accept all answers.)
*What other ways do people make music? (People often use musical
nstruments, which include pianos, drums, trumpets, clarinets, and
any more. People can make all sorts of sounds with a musical instru-
ent, just by blowing or moving their hands.)*

EL FLORÓN (THE FLOWER)
Kinesthetic Learning: The "El florón" Game

lorón means "the flower." The song is part of a game from
xico. To play the game, first have children make flowers out of
ue paper. Then, have children stand in a circle, with their hands
n behind their backs. Appoint one child to be "It". As the song
ys, It walks around the outside of the circle, pretending to put a
er flower in each child's hands. At some point, It does put the
ver in a child's hands, but then continues to pretend as before.
en the song ends, It goes to the center of the circle and asks three
ldren to guess who has the flower. The child who guesses correctly
omes the new It. If no one guesses correctly, the child who was It
s another turn.

EL BARCO CHIQUITITO (THE LITTLE BOAT)
Science Background

ats can be made of all sorts of things, including wood, plastic,
d metal. If you put a piece of metal in water, however, it would
k to the bottom. So, why do boats float? The answer is that the
pe of the boat keeps air in the middle. Air helps keep the boat
ove water.

ople use ships and boats to move things over water. In some
ce, like Venice, Italy, and the San Juan Islands of Washington

State, boats are the only way to move from island to island. People
also ride in boats just for fun.

Have children find information about different kinds of boats in
encyclopedias or other books, or the Internet. Ask them to share
what they learn with the class.

37. CADA VEZ QUE NOS JUNTAMOS
(See 20. The More We Get Together.)

38. CORRE TRENECITO CORRE
(See 10. Down at the Station)

39. TODOS LOS NACIDOS EN ENERO
Mathematics Connection

On the chalkboard, write down the names of the 12 months. Survey
the class to see how many of them were born in each of the months.
Record this information on the chalkboard.

DISCUSSION

- ¿Qué mes tiene el mayor número de cumpleaños? ¿Qué mes
  tiene el menor número de cumpleaños? (Hay varias respuestas
  posibles).
- Si dos personas tienen el mismo cumpleaños, ¿eso significa que
  son de la misma edad? (No. Pudieron haber nacido en años
  diferentes).
- *Which month had the most birthdays? Which month had the
  fewest birthdays? (Answers will vary)*
- *If two people have the same birthday, does that mean they're the
  same age? (No. They might have been born in different years.)*

41. LA MONTAÑA (THE MOUNTAIN)
Kinesthetic Learning

As children sing the song, have them make hand and arm gestures
to accompany the lyrics. For a rocky mountain, clasp hands high
overhead, to form a triangle shape. For a sunny valley, spread arms
widely, forming a broad "U" shape. For a stormy ocean, hold arms
horizontally in front of the body, and move them back and forth,
and up and down.

DISCUSSION

- ¿Han ido de paseo a las montañas alguna vez? ¿Qué les
  parecieron? (Acepte todas las respuestas).
- ¿Por qué podría resultarle difícil a la gente vivir en una mon-
  taña? (La edificación de casas y caminos por lo general resulta
  más difícil en las montañas empinadas que en las tierras planas.
  Además, el tiempo en las montañas puede cambiar muy rápida-
  mente).
- *Have you ever visited the mountains? What were they like?
  (Accept all answers.)*
- *Why might it be difficult for people to live on a mountain?
  (Building houses and roads is usually more difficult on steep mountains
  than on flatter lands. Also, the weather on mountains can change very
  quickly.)*

42. VAMOS A LA MAR (LET'S GO TO THE SEA)
(See 32. La mar estaba serena)

43. MI CUERPO (MY BODY)
(See 33. Hombros y cabeza)